The Joy of Organ Music

The Joy Of Organ Music embodies a colorful well-balanced repertoire of easy to play melodies. Of particular interest are the familiar themes by the masters, folk tunes, favorite standard songs and popular melodies of today.

The skillfull, full-sounding arrangements by Nelson Varon are intended for the beginning or early-intermediate grade player; they are most appealing in their simplicity and interesting enough to prepare and inspire the player for more advanced study.

Suggested registrations are found at the beginning of each piece with additional general instructions on Page 3.

© 1967 Yorktown Music Press, Inc.
33 West 60th Street New York 10023

Music Sales Limited, 78 Newman Street, London W I
International Standard Book Number 0-8256-8007-7

Contents

INSTRUCTIONS FOR USING
ALL ORGAN REGISTRATIONS

I. Electronic Organs:

When registration calls for a stop which is not on your particular electronic organ use a similar sounding stop in the *same footage*. For example, if the registration calls for an 8′ String and your organ does not have a stop called String—use a Violin 8′, or Viola 8′, or Salicional 8′ etc.

II. Hammond Pre-Set Console Models:
Permanently set as follows:

UPPER Ⓑ and LOWER A♯

and use Drawbar registrations as indicated

III. M-100 and L-100 Hammond Spinet Models:
Set the tablets permanently as follows:

M-100 SERIES

PEDAL	PERCUSSION	VIBRATO	LOWER MANUAL	UPPER MANUAL	REV.	VOL.

L-100 SERIES

LOWER	UPPER	PERCUSSION	VIBRATO	REV.	VOL.

and use Drawbar registrations for Upper and Lower manuals and for Pedal as indicated at each selection.

IV. On all Hammond Spinet Models:

Disregard parenthesized numerals when you do not have that drawbar on your model organ, but *use* the paranthesized numeral if your model spinet *does* have the additional Drawbar.

Fascination

ELECTRONIC ORGANS
Upper: String 8′
Lower: Melodia 8′

Pedal: 8′
Vibrato: On Full

DRAWBAR ORGANS
Upper: 00 8222-232
Lower: (00) 4302-000 (0)

Pedal: 3 (2)
Vibrato: On Full

Slow Waltz

Filippo D. Marchetti

Parade Of The Tin Soldiers

ELECTRONIC ORGANS
Upper: Trumpet 8′
Lower: Diapason 8′
Pedal: 8′
Vibrato: On Full

DRAWBAR ORGANS
Upper: 00-7677-540
Lower: (00)-5431-210 (0)
Pedal: 4 (3)
Vibrato: On Full

Leon Jessel

Lively walking tempo

Moscow Nights

ELECTRONIC ORGANS
Upper: Trumpet 8′   Pedal: 8′
Lower: Diapason 8′   Vibrato: On Full

DRAWBAR ORGANS
Upper: 00-7677-540   Pedal: 4 (3)
Lower: (00)-5431-210 (0)   Vibrato: On Full

V. Soloviev - Sedoy

The Whistler And His Dog

ELECTRONIC ORGANS
Upper: Flute 8′   Pedal: 8′
Lower: Melodia 8′   Vibrato: On Full

DRAWBAR ORGANS
Upper: 008200-000   Pedal: 3 (2)
Lower: (00) 4302-000 (0)   Vibrato: On Full

Arthur Pryor

Moderate walking tempo

Estrellita

ELECTRONIC ORGANS
Upper: String 8′
Lower: Melodia 8′
Pedal: 8′
Vibrato: On Full

DRAWBAR ORGANS
Upper: 00 8222-232
Lower: (00) 4302-000 (0)
Pedal: 3 (2)
Vibrato: On Full

Manuel M. Ponce

Slowly, with feeling

Clarinet Polka

ELECTRONIC ORGANS
Upper: Clarinet 8′   Pedal: 8′
Lower: Melodia 8′   Vibrato: On Full

DRAWBAR ORGANS
Upper: 00-8040-400   Pedal 3 (2)
Lower: (00) 43-03-000 (0)   Vibrato: On Full

Traditional

Elegie

ELECTRONIC ORGANS
Upper: Clarinet 8′
Lower: Melodia 8′

Pedal: 8′
Vibrato: On Full

DRAWBAR ORGANS
Upper: 00-8040-400
Lower: (00) 43-03-000 (0)

Pedal 3 (2)
Vibrato: On Full

Jules Massenet

Slowly

Adios Muchachos

ELECTRONIC ORGANS
Upper: Flutes 16′, 8′ 4′
       Strings 8′
       Reed 8′
Lower: Melodia 8′
       Diapason 8′

Pedal: 16′, 8′
Vibrato: On Full

DRAWBAR ORGANS
Upper: 60-8856-364
Lower: (00) 6523-454 (0)

Pedal: 6 (4)
Vibrato: On Full

Julio Sanders

Moderate Tango

Arkansas Traveler

ELECTRONIC ORGANS
Upper: String 8′ Pedal: 8′
Lower: Melodia 8′ Vibrato: On Full

DRAWBAR ORGANS
Upper: 00 8222-232 Pedal: 3 (2)
Lower: (00) 4302-000 (0) Vibrato: On Full

Traditional

A Touch Of Blues

ELECTRONIC ORGANS
Upper: String 8′   Pedal: 8′
Lower: Melodia 8′   Vibrato: On Full

DRAWBAR ORGANS
Upper: 00 8222-232   Pedal: 3 (2)
Lower: (00) 4302-000 (0)   Vibrato: On Full

Gerald Martin

Slow, lazy beat

Boogie Woogie Martian Star

ELECTRONIC ORGANS
Upper: Flutes 16′, 8′ 4′   Pedal: 16′, 8′
      Strings 8′   Vibrato: On Full
      Reed 8′
Lower: Melodia 8′
      Diapason 8′

DRAWBAR ORGANS
Upper: 60-8856-364   Pedal: 6 (4)
Lower: (00) 6523-454 (0)   Vibrato: On Full

Nelson Varon

Moderately, with a strong beat

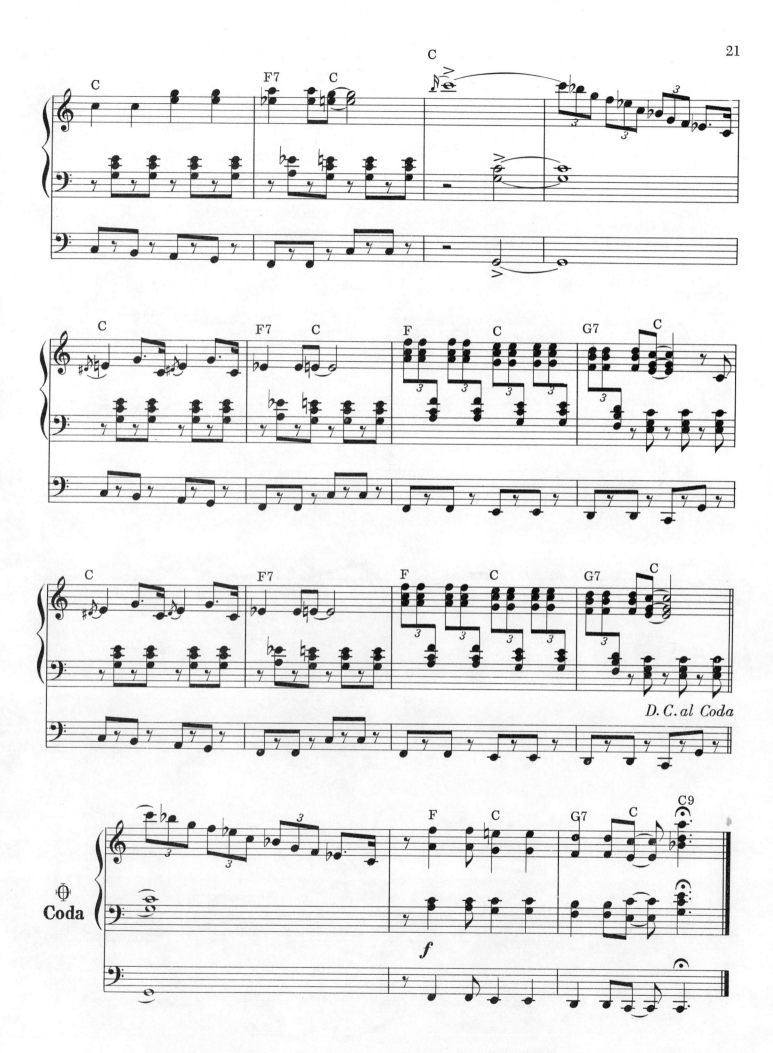

Chicken Reel

ELECTRONIC ORGANS
Upper: String 8′   Pedal: 8′
Lower: Melodia 8′   Vibrato: On Full

DRAWBAR ORGANS
Upper: 00 8222-232   Pedal: 3 (2)
Lower: (00) 4302-000 (0)   Vibrato: On Full

Lively

Traditional

The Cowboy's Lament

(The Streets of Laredo)

ELECTRONIC ORGANS
Upper: Trumpet 8′
Lower: Diapason 8′
Pedal: 8′
Vibrato: On Full

DRAWBAR ORGANS
Upper: 00-7677-540
Lower: (00)-5431-210 (0)
Pedal: 4 (3)
Vibrato: On Full

Folk Song

Moderately

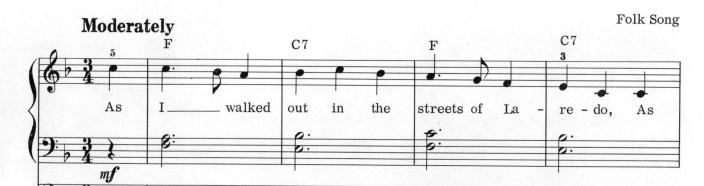

As I ____ walked out in the streets of La - re - do, As

I walked out in La - re - do one day, I

spied a poor cow - boy, all wrapped in white lin - en, All

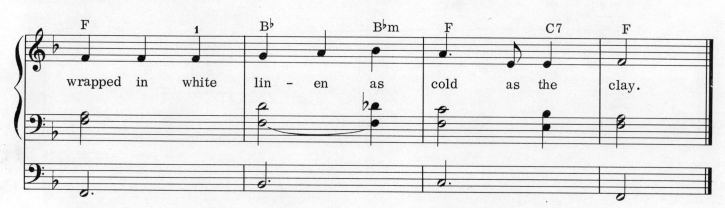

wrapped in white lin - en as cold as the clay.

Londonderry Air

ELECTRONIC ORGANS
Upper: Flute 8′
Lower: Melodia 8′
Pedal: 8′
Vibrato: On Full

DRAWBAR ORGANS
Upper: 008200-000
Lower: (00) 4302-000 (0)
Pedal: 3 (2)
Vibrato: On Full

Irish Song

Down In The Valley

ELECTRONIC ORGANS
Upper: Flute 8′ Pedal: 8′
Lower: Melodia 8′ Vibrato: On Full

DRAWBAR ORGANS
Upper: 008200-000 Pedal: 3 (2)
Lower: (00) 4302-000 (0) Vibrato: On Full

Gently moving

Folk Song

Down in the val - ley, val - ley so low,

Hang your head o - ver, Hear the wind blow.

Hear the wind blow, love, Hear the wind blow,

Hang your head ov - er, Hear the wind blow.

Marian

ELECTRONIC ORGANS
Upper: Trumpet 8'   Pedal: 8'
Lower: Diapason 8'   Vibrato: On Full

DRAWBAR ORGANS
Upper: 00-7677-540   Pedal: 4 (3)
Lower: (00)-5431-210 (0)   Vibrato: On Full

Moderate

Calypso Song

All day, all night, Ma-ri-an, Down by sea-side sift-ing sand.

Ev-'ry-one loves Ma-ri-an, Down by sea-side sift-ing sand.

Fine

Why don't you come down to Tri-ni-dad; You'll have the best time you ev-er had.

'Cause ev-'ry-thing is so ver-y nice, Come on and see this is-land par-a-dise.

D.C. al Fine

Greensleeves

ELECTRONIC ORGANS
Upper: String 8'   Pedal: 8'
Lower: Melodia 8'   Vibrato: On Full

DRAWBAR ORGANS
Upper: 00 8222-232   Pedal: 3 (2)
Lower: (00) 4302-000 (0)   Vibrato: On Full

Moderately

English Folk Song

Careless Love

ELECTRONIC ORGANS
Upper: Clarinet 8'   Pedal: 8'
Lower: Melodia 8'   Vibrato: On Full

DRAWBAR ORGANS
Upper: 00-8040-400   Pedal 3 (2)
Lower: (00) 43-03-000 (0)   Vibrato: On Full

Moderately

Folk Song

Lullaby

ELECTRONIC ORGANS
Upper: Flute 8′   Pedal: 8′
Lower: Melodia 8′   Vibrato: On Full

DRAWBAR ORGANS
Upper: 008200-000   Pedal: 3 (2)
Lower: (00) 4302-000 (0)   Vibrato: On Full

Johannes Brahms

Hungarian Dance No. 4

ELECTRONIC ORGANS
Upper: String 8′ Pedal: 8′
Lower: Melodia 8′ Vibrato: On Full

DRAWBAR ORGANS
Upper: 00 8222-232 Pedal: 3 (2)
Lower: (00) 4302-000 (0) Vibrato: On Full

Johannes Brahms

Träumerei

ELECTRONIC ORGANS
Upper: String 8′   Pedal: 8′
Lower: Melodia 8′   Vibrato: On Full

DRAWBAR ORGANS
Upper: 00 8222-232   Pedal: 3 (2)
Lower: (00) 4302-000 (0)   Vibrato: On Full

Robert Schumann

Slowly, with feeling

Waltz

ELECTRONIC ORGANS
Upper: Clarinet 8' Pedal: 8'
Lower: Melodia 8' Vibrato: On Full

DRAWBAR ORGANS
Upper: 00-8040-400 Pedal 3 (2)
Lower: (00) 43-03-000 (0) Vibrato: On Full

Slowly

Johannes Brahms

Pomp and Circumstance

ELECTRONIC ORGANS
Upper: Flutes 16′, 8′ 4′
      Strings 8′
      Reed 8′
Lower: Melodia 8′
      Diapason 8′

Pedal: 16′, 8′
Vibrato: On Full

DRAWBAR ORGANS
Upper: 60-8856-364
Lower: (00) 6523-454 (0)

Pedal: 6 (4)
Vibrato: On Full

Edward Elgar

Broadly

Sheep May Safely Graze

ELECTRONIC ORGANS
Upper: Trumpet 8′   Pedal: 8′
Lower: Diapason 8′   Vibrato: On Full

DRAWBAR ORGANS
Upper: 00-7677-540   Pedal: 4 (3)
Lower: (00)-5431-210 (0)   Vibrato: On Full

Gently moving

Johann Sebastian Bach

Arioso

ELECTRONIC ORGANS
Upper: String 8'   Pedal: 8'
Lower: Melodia 8'   Vibrato: On Full

DRAWBAR ORGANS
Upper: 00 8222-232   Pedal: 3 (2)
Lower: (00) 4302-000 (0)   Vibrato: On Full

Johann Sebastian Bach

Nocturne

ELECTRONIC ORGANS
Upper: String 8′   Pedal: 8′
Lower: Melodia 8′   Vibrato: On Full

DRAWBAR ORGANS
Upper: 00 8222-232   Pedal: 3 (2)
Lower: (00) 4302-000 (0) Vibrato: On Full

Slowly, with expression

Frederic Chopin

Clair De Lune

ELECTRONIC ORGANS
Upper: Flute 8'   Pedal: 8'
Lower: Melodia 8'   Vibrato: On Full

DRAWBAR ORGANS
Upper: 008200-000   Pedal: 3 (2)
Lower: (00) 4302-000 (0)   Vibrato: On Full

Slowly, with expression

Claude Debussy

Theme from "Pathetique Symphony"

ELECTRONIC ORGANS
Upper: String 8′
Lower: Melodia 8′
Pedal: 8′
Vibrato: On Full

DRAWBAR ORGANS
Upper: 00 8222-232
Lower: (00) 4302-000 (0)
Pedal: 3 (2)
Vibrato: On Full

Peter I. Tchaikovsky

Moderately, with expression

I Love Thee

ELECTRONIC ORGANS
Upper: Clarinet 8′   Pedal: 8′
Lower: Melodia 8′   Vibrato: On Full

DRAWBAR ORGANS
Upper: 00-8040-400   Pedal 3 (2)
Lower: (00) 43-03-000 (0)   Vibrato: On Full

Edvard Grieg

Slowly, with expression

Ave Maria

ELECTRONIC ORGANS
Upper: String 8′   Pedal: 8′
Lower: Melodia 8′   Vibrato: On Full

DRAWBAR ORGANS
Upper: 00 8222-232   Pedal: 3 (2)
Lower: (00) 4302-000 (0)   Vibrato: On Full

Bach - Gounod

My Heart At Thy Sweet Voice

from "Samson and Delilah"

ELECTRONIC ORGANS
Upper: Flute 8′ Pedal: 8′
Lower: Melodia 8′ Vibrato: On Full

DRAWBAR ORGANS
Upper: 008200-000 Pedal: 3 (2)
Lower: (00) 4302-000 (0) Vibrato: On Full

Camille Saint - Saens

Moderately

To A Wild Rose

ELECTRONIC ORGANS
Upper: Flute 8'   Pedal: 8'
Lower: Melodia 8'   Vibrato: On Full

DRAWBAR ORGANS
Upper: 008200-000   Pedal: 3 (2)
Lower: (00) 4302-000 (0) Vibrato: On Full

Edward MacDowell

With simple tenderness

Musetta's Waltz

from "La Boheme"

ELECTRONIC ORGANS
Upper: String 8'   Pedal: 8'
Lower: Melodia 8'   Vibrato: On Full

DRAWBAR ORGANS
Upper: 00 8222-232   Pedal: 3 (2)
Lower: (00) 4302-000 (0)   Vibrato: On Full

Giacomo Puccini

The Emperor Waltz

ELECTRONIC ORGANS
Upper: Flutes 16′, 8′ 4′
      Strings 8′
      Reed 8′
Lower: Melodia 8′
      Diapason 8′

Pedal: 16′, 8′
Vibrato: On Full

DRAWBAR ORGANS
Upper: 60-8856-364
Lower: (00) 6523-454 (0)

Pedal: 6 (4)
Vibrato: On Full

Johann Strauss

Saint Anthony Chorale

ELECTRONIC ORGANS
Upper: Flutes 16′, 8′   Pedal: 16′
        String 8′   Vibrato: Off
Lower: Diapason 8′

DRAWBAR ORGANS
Upper: 40-5545-336   Pedal: 4 (3)
Lower: (00) 5500-320 (0)   Vibrato: Off

Joseph Haydn

Moderately

Comedians' Galop

ELECTRONIC ORGANS
Upper: Trumpet 8′
Lower: Diapason 8′
Pedal: 8′
Vibrato: On Full

DRAWBAR ORGANS
Upper: 00-7677-540
Lower: (00)-5431-210 (0)
Pedal: 4 (3)
Vibrato: On Full

Very bright

Dmitri Kabalevsky

Notturno
Theme from String Quartet No. 2

ELECTRONIC ORGANS
Upper: Flute 8' Pedal: 8'
Lower: Melodia 8' Vibrato: On Full

DRAWBAR ORGANS
Upper: 008200-000 Pedal: 3 (2)
Lower: (00) 4302-000 (0) Vibrato: On Full

Alexander Borodin

Mighty Lak' A Rose

ELECTRONIC ORGANS
Upper: Clarinet 8'   Pedal: 8'
Lower: Melodia 8'   Vibrato: On Full

DRAWBAR ORGANS
Upper: 00-8040-400   Pedal 3 (2)
Lower: (00) 43-03-000 (0)   Vibrato.. On Full

Ethelbert Nevin

Slowly and gently

D. C. al Fine

Kiss Me Again

ELECTRONIC ORGANS
Upper: Flutes 16', 8'
      String 8'
Lower: Diapason 8'

Pedal: 16'
Vibrato: Off

DRAWBAR ORGANS
Upper: 40-5545-336
Lower: (00) 5500-320 (0)

Pedal: 4 (3)
Vibrato: Off

Slow waltz

Victor Herbert

Sweet sum - mer - breeze, whis - per - ing trees,

Stars shin - ing soft - ly a - bove;

Ros - es in bloom, waft - ed per - fume,

Sleep - y birds dream - ing of love.

Look Down That Lonesome Road

ELECTRONIC ORGANS
Upper: Flutes 16', 8'
    String 8'
Lower: Diapason 8'
Pedal: 16'
Vibrato: Off

DRAWBAR ORGANS
Upper: 40-5545-336
Lower: (00) 5500-320 (0)
Pedal: 4 (3)
Vibrato: Off

Traditional

On The Banks Of The Wabash

ELECTRONIC ORGANS
Upper: Clarinet 8′   Pedal: 8′
Lower: Melodia 8′   Vibrato: On Full

DRAWBAR ORGANS
Upper: 00-8040-400   Pedal 3 (2)
Lower: (00) 43-03-000 (0)   Vibrato: On Full

Paul Dresser

Deep River

ELECTRONIC ORGANS
Upper: String 8′   Pedal: 8′
Lower: Melodia 8′   Vibrato: On Full

DRAWBAR ORGANS
Upper: 00 8222-232   Pedal: 3 (2)
Lower: (00) 4302-000 (0)   Vibrato: On Full

Slowly

Spiritual

D.C. al Fine

Nobody Knows The Trouble I've Seen

ELECTRONIC ORGANS
Upper: Flutes 16′, 8′ 4′   Pedal: 16′, 8′
      Strings 8′   Vibrato: On Full
      Reed 8′
Lower: Melodia 8′
      Diapason 8′

DRAWBAR ORGANS
Upper: 60-8856-364   Pedal: 6 (4)
Lower: (00) 6523-454 (0)   Vibrato: On Full

Slowly

Spiritual

Lyrics:

No-bo-dy knows the troub-le I've seen, No-bo-dy knows but Je-sus.

No-bo-dy knows the troub-le I've seen, Glo-ry hal-le-lu-jah!

Fine

Some-times I'm up, some-times I'm down; Oh, yes, Lord; Some-

times I'm al-most to the ground, Oh, yes, Lord.

D.C. al Fine

Yankee Doodle Dandy

ELECTRONIC ORGANS
Upper: Flutes 16', 8' 4'
        Strings 8'
        Reed 8'
Lower: Melodia 8'
        Diapason 8'

Pedal: 16', 8'
Vibrato: On Full

DRAWBAR ORGANS
Upper: 60-8856-364
Lower: (00) 6523-454 (0)

Pedal: 6 (4)
Vibrato: On Full

Lively

George M. Cohan

69

In The Good Old Summertime

ELECTRONIC ORGANS
Upper: Flutes 16′, 8′ 4′
      Strings 8′
      Reed 8′
Lower: Melodia 8′
      Diapason 8′

Pedal: 16′, 8′
Vibrato: On Full

DRAWBAR ORGANS
Upper: 60-8856-364
Lower: (00) 6523-454 (0)

Pedal: 6 (4)
Vibrato: On Full

Ren Shields

George Evans

Merry waltz tempo

In the good old sum — mer time, In the good old sum — mer time, Stroll — ing thro' the shad — y lanes With your ba — by mine;

Vilia

from "The Merry Widow"

ELECTRONIC ORGANS
Upper: Clarinet 8′   Pedal: 8′
Lower: Melodia 8′   Vibrato: On Full

DRAWBAR ORGANS
Upper: 00-8040-400   Pedal 3 (2)
Lower: (00) 43-03-000 (0)   Vibrato: On Full

Franz Lehar

Moderately

Vi - lia, my Vi - lia, I love on - ly thee,
And in thy eyes lies the whole world for me.
Life here be - low would be oh, so di - vine
If I could just make you mine.

Wait Till The Sun Shines Nellie

ELECTRONIC ORGANS
Upper: Flutes 16', 8' 4'
      Strings 8'
      Reed 8'
Lower: Melodia 8'
      Diapason 8'

Pedal: 16', 8'
Vibrato: On Full

DRAWBAR ORGANS
Upper: 60-8856-364
Lower: (00) 6523-454 (0)

Pedal: 6 (4)
Vibrato: On Full

Andrew B. Sterling

Harry Von Tilzer

Lively

Hello My Baby

ELECTRONIC ORGANS
Upper: Flutes 16′, 8′ 4′   Pedal: 16′, 8′
      Strings 8′   Vibrato: On Full
      Reed 8′
Lower: Melodia 8′
      Diapason 8′

DRAWBAR ORGANS
Upper: 60-8856-364   Pedal: 6 (4)
Lower: (00) 6523-454 (0)   Vibrato: On Full

Howard and Emerson

Lively ragtime

America, The Beautiful

ELECTRONIC ORGANS
Upper: Flutes 16', 8'   Pedal: 16'
          String 8'   Vibrato: Off
Lower: Diapason 8'

DRAWBAR ORGANS
Upper: 40-5545-336   Pedal: 4 (3)
Lower: (00) 5500-320 (0)   Vibrato: Off

Katherine L. Bates

Samuel A. Ward

With pride

Thanksgiving Hymn

ELECTRONIC ORGANS
Upper: Flutes 16', 8'   Pedal: 16'
     String 8'   Vibrato: Off
Lower: Diapason 8'

DRAWBAR ORGANS
Upper: 40-5545-336   Pedal: 4 (3)
Lower: (00) 5500-320 (0)   Vibrato: Off

Moderately

Traditional Dutch Air

We gath-er to-geth-er to ask the Lord's bless-ing, He chast-ens and hast-ens His will to make known; The wick-ed op-press-ing now cease them from dis-tress-ing, Sing prais-es to His name,___ He for-gets not His own.

O Come All Ye Faithful

(Adeste Fideles)

ELECTRONIC ORGANS
Upper: Flutes 16', 8'   Pedal: 16'
String 8'   Vibrato: Off
Lower: Diapason 8'

DRAWBAR ORGANS
Upper: 40-5545-336   Pedal: 4 (3)
Lower: (00) 5500-320 (0)   Vibrato: Off

Traditional

Auld Lang Syne

ELECTRONIC ORGANS
Upper: Flutes 16', 8' 4'   Pedal: 16', 8'
       Strings 8'   Vibrato: On Full
       Reed 8'
Lower: Melodia 8'
       Diapason 8'

DRAWBAR ORGANS
Upper: 60-8856-364   Pedal: 6 (4)
Lower: (00) 6523-454 (0)   Vibrato: On Full

Scotch Air